1

NAKED TEXT

Email Writing Skills for Teenagers

Copyright 2015 by Gisela Hausmann

Published by Educ-Easy Books
POB 6366, Greenville, SC 29606

* * *

ISBN:
978-0-9963893-8-9

***

Editor:
Divya Lavanya

Cover Design:
Gisela Hausmann

***

Copyright Attributions/via Shutterstock
Young Asian Woman in a park texting by blvdone
Black Smartphone by Denis Semenchenko
social media design by gst
Treehouse in Paris cente by Ewan Chesser
avatars by Toonstyle .com

***

Please note:

Throughout this book, the pronoun "he" is used with intended gender-neutral meaning, as "he" has been used traditionally in English. Whenever you read "he," I could be referring to a man or woman. Unless noted otherwise, I protect the privacy of others, which in this book includes not even revealing the person's gender.

The depicted avatars are a visualization of the same concept. The avatars too are to be understood with intended gender-neutral meaning, as "he" has been used traditionally in English.

Please also note: The featured e-mails are 'based' on true e-mails.

Some names and identifying details have been omitted as they are not relevant.

***

Table of Contents

***

TEXTING VS. WRITING E-MAILS

Thank you for selecting my book to help you write the best and most effective e-mails you can. Regardless of what you want to do for the rest of your life, this skill will serve you well.

Maybe you don't even like writing e-mails because you like texting better. Texting is faster; it allows you to add pictures instantly; plus, you can make your message more interesting by adding emoticons.

If that is how you feel about texting – you are not alone. According to a Nielsen Mobile report, already in 2009 Americans sent more text messages than they made phone calls. In 2012, seventeen-year old Austin Wierschke from Wisconsin won $50,000 by capturing his second straight title at the LG Electronics' 2012 U.S. National Texting Championship. He texted 149 characters in 39 seconds with no spelling or punctuation errors. The original pool of hopefuls numbered more than 100,000 young people.

So, yes, I see your point.

Sending text messages is great when communicating with friends or people you know well. However, if you want to do big things in life, you'll probably need to send e-mails. All people of influence communicate this way.

Did you know that even the late visionary and genius Steve Jobs read many Apple Inc. customers' e-mails and replied to them – personally? Jobs' e-mail address was no secret, he had it published on the web.

http://www.maclife.com/article/gallery/10_best_steve_jobs_e mails_ever

Not surprisingly, Steve Jobs also exchanged e-mails with Google's CEO Eric Schmidt because power players communicate via e-mail.

http://www.emailsfromstevejobs.com/2012/01/28/court-filings-show-steve-jobs-told-google-to-stop-poaching-apple-engineers/

You probably also heard about Mrs. Hillary Clinton's issues regarding the e-mails she sent during her time as United States' Secretary of State. While I am not going to comment on that topic, the point is, government officials as well as CIA and FBI agents send important and classified information – via e-mail.

Generally speaking, important information is always transmitted via e-mail and at the same time the reverse is true too: If you send information via e-mail it makes the information look more important than if you would send only a text message.

Texting expresses who you are now and what you are doing "in the now."

E-mail can help you to express who you are going to be and what you are going to do "in the future."

YOUR PLANS FOR THE FUTURE

Of course, you already know that to achieve big goals most often you need to team up with others. Whether your plan is to get into a specific college or to found a start-up company, or even to become a rock star or a painter, you will have to connect with people who can and want to help. This process is called networking.

Networking [net-wur-king] noun

: a supportive system of sharing information and services among individuals and groups having a common interest

Almost always, your parents will be in your corner but often you will also need the help of specialists, who are experts in their respective fields.

Sometimes, finding experts who can and will help is easy.

High schools and colleges have counselors who can assist with information and advice on any aspect of student life. Still, eventually, you'll need to apply for a job by sending a cover letter and a resume – via e-mail.

Similarly, if you are an aspiring athlete, you'll be able to get help from your school's coaches.

If, however, you intend to found a start-up company, you will need partners and financiers. They are not readily available.

To get them aboard, you'll need to send them e-mails, which showcase your ideas and concepts. Most often you'll get only one shot, so your first e-mail has to be good, really good.

Even people who work mostly alone and who may not need major start-up money need to make favorable connections. For instance, an artist, who mostly draws or paints alone in his studio apartment, needs an agent who represents him and who arranges exhibitions at galleries as well as media coverage for these events. A good agent is any artist's most important team member.

*

Very often, the difference between being a professional and being a successful professional depends only on the number of successful connections you can create.

*

One of the easiest ways to create a connection with a person you previously did not know is to send an **outstanding, creative, and hopefully even remarkable** e-mail.

Everybody wants to know the person who will shine in the future. You can be this person.

TRYING TO REACH INFLUENCERS

To illustrate the power and greatness of e-mail I need to go back in time a bit and explain how things used to be, about twenty years ago.

1. In those days every person of influence had a secretary. Not only CEO's and department managers, everybody who was in charge of only five to ten people had a secretary. Even university professors had secretaries, who answered the phone, opened letters, and made appointments. These secretaries were incredibly powerful; they were the guards of their bosses' doors, not virtually but literally. It was in their power to put a letter at the bottom of the stack, and they could deem business letters "unimportant." If you wanted to reach any influencer you had to get past these guards. I probably don't have to mention that most often this wasn't easy.

[influencer, *[in•flu•enc•er \-sə(r)\]*
noun
: one that influences

to influence, *[in•floo•uh ns]* verb
(used with object),
: to exercise influence on; affect; sway: to influence a person.
: to move or impel (a person) to some action

2. In the olden days, "looks" counted, too. Many influential people, but also their secretaries, judged business letters and proposals by their appearances. That meant, to impress you had to write business letters on hand-made paper or special stationary with golden imprint, and sign it

with a fountain pen. Things could get expensive pretty quickly.

3. Naturally, even then, a letter or a proposal alone could not always express every business idea in all details. Typically, pictures, graphics, and tables help to illustrate new concepts. But, in the "olden days" people used typewriters which could not produce graphics or print pictures. Therefore, business people needed to hire graphic artists who designed brochures, and then had them printed. Entrepreneurs who wanted to include a video even had to hire a professional video crew. Start-up costs could be quite high.

The only reason why people did all of these things was because they wanted to look like attractive, already somewhat successful business people, so the gatekeeper/ secretary would pass on their proposal to the influencer they wanted to get in touch with. Without getting past the gatekeeper/watchdog, entrepreneurs could not make the connection, in those days.

Obviously, today all these difficulties are gone. Everybody can design awesome-looking presentations, shoot videos from their smartphones and put together an impressive presentation, which can be attached to an e-mail with the click of a button.

In other words – it's all about composing the contact e-mail!

THE GLORIOUS NEWS:
THE WATCH DOGS ARE GONE!

Today, many well-known and even famous influencers don't have secretaries any longer; they open and read their e-mails themselves – **IF** the subject line intrigues them.

I already mentioned that even Steve Jobs did that.

*

The good news is, opposite to twenty years ago getting the attention of an influencer is only one (1) e-mail away – one well-written e-mail!

> The bad news is, for that very reason, too many people try to get the attention of the same influencers. Many influencers receive hundreds or even thousands of e-mails per day.

The good news is that all e-mails look basically the same. There is no need for buying a special stationary or signing with a fountain pen. CONTENT RULES!

> The bad news is that many people focus only on their project and not on how to present their project best to others. Some people write run-of-the-mill, boring, and uncreative e-mails. Writing e-mails to pitch potential partners or influencers needs to be considered marketing, and no efforts should be spared.

More good news is that since everybody hates run-of-the-mill, boring, and uncreative e-mails, the senders of the most remarkable, interesting e-mails can get through to anybody, even to the most important influencer in their field!

*

That is the reason why I hope you will study this book inside and out, read it twice, and write all your e-mails with the utmost care, always knowing that every single e-mail can catapult you not only where you want to be but even farther than you ever dreamed you could go.

E-mail is THE GREAT EQUALIZER
– The person who can make his case best (not the person who went to the best university or who has the most money) will come out on top.

PRACTICAL APPLICATIONS & E-MAIL IS A TOOL

At this point you probably agree with me that writing best e-mails can be very useful. But, you might wonder what to do with this knowledge right now, when you are still in school.

E-mail is a tool, just like a hammer. You can take a hammer and nail two boards together or you can build a fantastic tree house. Your only limitation is the amount of energy and efforts you want to put into pursuing your plan(s).

This book is a non-fluff, no-nonsense book. You can apply everything you learn as soon as you have finished reading.

If at this time you only e-mail homework assignments to your teachers, please expand on it. Write e-mails to influencers and ask them to help you!

Maybe you are the president of a school club that is doing a fundraiser for a good cause. E-mail the morning news anchor of your local TV station and request to present your cause on the news!

A great e-mail might get the anchor's attention, and he might invite you to talk about your event on the news! This would probably help boost your fundraiser's revenue and at the same time you are adding a phenomenal project to your resume.

Maybe you are a blogger and you would like to invite an influencer to guest blog a few lines. Send him an e-mail and ask for it.

Maybe you are a programmer who would like to get a summer job or an internship at a specific company rather than working any job that really doesn't interest you or further your career plans. Check out the websites of the corporations you admire; then send an e-mail to their human resources department.

You will notice quickly what a great tool e-mail really is. Good e-mails open the doors to wherever you want to go.

So, let's find out how to do it.

THE 7 PARTS OF AN E-MAIL

The best way to compose a fantastic e-mail is to write a first draft and then improve each of these seven elements.

If your e-mail is a really important e-mail, you should go over it at least three times, every time looking for even the tiniest improvement. Maybe you are rolling your eyes now but always remember – people who have influence are looking for the interesting message...

Imagine being the recipient of the e-mail you are about to write. Then, imagine you are looking at about 100 e-mails in your Inbox. Which one will you open first? Probably, the one that looks most interesting.

*

"You must write the e-mail others will read."
- Gisela Hausmann

*

These are the 7 parts of an e-mail:

#1 – The sender's (your) name

#2 – The best time to send an e-mail

#3 – The attractive & effective subject line

#4 – The greeting

#5 – The spelling of the recipient's name

#6 – The body of your e-mail

#7 – The ending salutation & signature

#1 –THE SENDER'S (YOUR) NAME

Obviously, the sender's name is the most important part of any e-mail. All of us care mostly about the e-mails from people we like or from people who are significant in our lives.

If you found an e-mail from a sender "Pontifex @Vatican" in your Inbox, you'd immediately wonder if the sender is really the Pope or if this might be a phishing e-mail – You would not simply delete the message; you would wonder about it.

Maybe you'd even take a picture of "Pontifex's" e-mail and text it to all your friends and ask what they think.

That's the power of a name.

However, you don't have to be really famous to get people to want to open your e-mail first. In life all of us get hundreds of chances to create a name for ourselves and to build our reputation. Here is a story you'll be able to relate to.

*

From 2000–2002, I taught a freshman class called "Careers" at a high school in South Florida. This was a nine-week course, created to teach high school students how to apply for a job. Every nine weeks between 29 and 33 new students walked into my classroom; since they were freshmen, I did not know any of them.

On the first day of the course, I told my new students that I had no intention to find out if any of them had had pulled a silly prank in middle school or what grades they used to have in the past; they would be in charge of building their own reputation in my class.

Naturally, since I taught four of these courses per year, I had a hard time remembering the students' names. I told

19

them that and also, "You don't want to be the first student whose name I remember, unless you are aiming for being the best student in this class."

All of us remember the remarkable and the outstanding first, the good and – the bad.

Of course, two weeks after the course started, I knew all of my students' names. But, what about – today?

There are about a dozen students whose work I still remember – clearly and in detail. Even fifteen years later, I know what projects these students presented, how they scored, and should one of them, a student with the initials AW, ever run for president, I'll be the first one to say, "I knew it then!"

*

Equally, in fifteen years from now, many people will remember you. Every day, you make contacts, who will – or won't – remember you. The choice is yours!

As you grow older, you might encounter difficult situations like most of us do. Even with hardest work you may not be able to avoided mishaps. Sometimes you may even feel powerless. But, there is one thing you'll always own – your name!

If you build your name and reputation according to your talents and best life principles nobody will be able to taint that, because it is your name, today we say "your brand."

So, go and create it!

Do you want to be this math whiz whose name people mention with that certain timbre of respect?

Or, that kid who always tinkers with electronics?

The nerdy programmer with the nickname "Gates"?

(I use the word "nerdy" with the deepest respect as I admire Bill Gates' achievements tremendously. Since I am a terrible typist, being able to use a personal computer has changed my life.)

Maybe you want to be the kid who started a recycle program at your school?

Or, the kid who reads stories to little first graders who cannot read many of the more difficult words yet?

The choice is yours, and nobody can take it from you.

While you are building this brand of yours, I recommend that simultaneously you build a profile at LinkedIn. It'll be a representation of your brand to colleges and the world of professionals.

In a bit I'll show you how to use this trick as a major advantage.

You must be over the age of fourteen (14) or older to open an account and create a free profile. Please find more information in LinkedIn's user agreement.

https://www.linkedin.com/legal/user-agreement

If you are over the age of sixteen, you should definitively have a profile because it will have a positive impact when you apply for college.

To keep things professional, you'll need a (first name)(last name) e-mail address at yahoo.com or gmail.com. Do not use a colorful e-mail address like rockstar@wherever.com or QueenBree@wherever.com.

If your name is already taken you could choose

- (first name) (dot) (last name)

- (first name) (initial) (last name)

- (first name) (dot) (initial) (dot) (last name)

- (last name) (dot) (first name)

- (Initial first name) (last name)

Always look twice when picking your handle. Years ago I read that a Mr. Manual Alware had been hired at a company whose computer system generated e-mail addresses following an (initial of first name) (last name) system, which led to Mr. Alware's e-mail address being malware@xyzcompany.com.

Maybe this story is a hoax, and maybe not, but it suggests to pay attention.

Also, I would advise against incorporating your birth year into your e-mail address. It's nobody's business, in what year you were born. Age discrimination still exists. You don't want to be excluded from an exciting opportunity because somebody decides that you are too young just by looking at your e-mail address. Let your resume and your professional profile do the talking.

***

Use your professional e-mail address when creating your profile at LinkedIn. LinkedIn works just like any other social media platform, only it's purely professional. Therefore, only post what will help your future career.

Here are some suggestions on what to put in your profile:

Maybe you are a member of one of your school's clubs, or
- serve in student government
- are a member of a theater group, band or art group,

- volunteer at a hospital or at an animal shelter
- are a contributor to any of your school's social media feeds, or
- work a part-time job (even babysitting counts)

profile URL

Notice that you can also add pictures to illustrate your achievements. Think of it as a brag book (picture collection).

Always keep in mind that this page is supposed to represent your brand. Obviously, it needs to have a different look if you want to study the law at Harvard than if you are a budding rock star with your own YouTube channel.

Once your profile looks good, put a link to it in your e-mail signature, for a professional look. (Copy your profile's URL right below your portrait.)

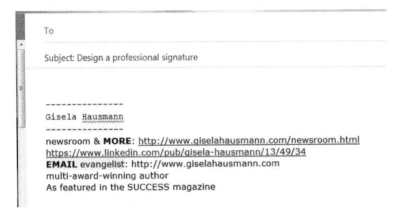

The closer you'll get to graduation, the more e-mails you'll have to write to college counselors and other professionals. Your new e-mail signature will make you look like a stand-out candidate.

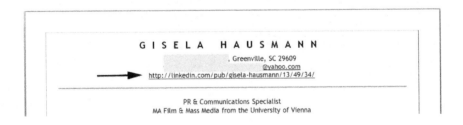

Also, include your Linkedin profile on any other professional paperwork. The benefit is that most often regular forms do not offer enough space for you to list all of your accomplishments. Your LinkedIn profile will serve as an "expanded resume."

#2 – THE BEST TIME TO SEND AN E-MAIL

You know this from texting – electronic communication is supposed to happen fast! Otherwise it's not cool! Most of us find it annoying when people do not respond within 24 hours.

If you know or guess that it will take more than twenty-four hours to put together the needed information, simply acknowledge the receipt of the e-mail and advise when the your recipient can expect your complete reply.

Replying with

"Dear ...xyz,
Thank you for sending me (e.g.) the attached admission forms. Please expect to receive all requested materials by ... (date).
As always,
(your name)

demonstrates professionalism.

#3 – THE ATTRACTIVE & EFFECTIVE SUBJECT LINE

Worldwide over 100 billion e-mails are sent every day. The Radicati Group, Inc, a Technology Market Research Firm, forecasts that by the end of 2017 over 132 billion e-mails will be sent and received per day!

Office workers spend about 11.2 hours or 28% of their workweek dealing with e-mails.

This equates to every office worker receiving about 100 e-mails per day, statistically.

During exam time your professors may receive many more e-mails per day, because they also receive e-mails from other faculty members and the administration.

With so many e-mails to choose from, typically, people open their e-mails based on two factors:

- the name of the sender
- the appeal of the subject line.

The most appealing subject lines offer

- precise information (who, what, when)
- an interesting pitch for a job application or business proposal
- a heart-felt thank-you

For instance, at a college where thousands of students are enrolled, it is quite possible that two or more students have the same or a very similar name. Therefore, any information which helps college professors, counselors, and other employees to do their job faster is considered to be "stand-out." No recipient wants to research who is who.

Consequently, any professor who receives an e-mail with the subject line

"BUS **121**, assignment term paper by John Smith"

will think of the student John Smith as a highly organized student.

Having analyzed 100,000+ e-mails, I can vouch for the fact that two types of characters will make any subject line stand out in any Inbox:

- numbers
- special signs (!, **?**, :, *)

Therefore, if possible always use a number, like your student ID number, the course number, or a date.
[Never ever use your social security number because identity theft is a huge problem.]

Here are more examples:

- Essay, homework assignment from **09/28/2014**
- CRJ **140** Term paper (student ID number)
- John Smith's homework September **28, 2014**
- Re: Final rehearsal for Christmas concert!

The same trick can also be used for all other e-mails.
For instance, if you write a complaint e-mail regarding a purchase, list the order number in the subject line.

- cancellation of order# **123456** dated **05/29/14**

There is no faster way to say "I mean business," than listing numbers. Only prepared, organized people list numbers, and vice versa, people who list numbers are organized.

If you decide to pitch your local newspaper or TV-station about an interesting school event, you could write

- **09/28 -** (your high school's initials)'s National Honor Society Fundraiser Event

On a job application:

- (your name), HS's **2015** Spelling Bee Winner is looking for a summer job to earn money for college

- **2 x** Science Fair Winner is looking for a summer job to earn money for college

- HS student with GPA **3.47** is looking for a summer job to earn money for college

To test the effectiveness of subject lines, send e-mails with various options you are pondering to yourself BEFORE you send it to your recipient.

Then, close your Inbox. Walk away and get some distance. After that, open your Inbox again. You will probably see right away which subject line stands out.

***

Lastly, there is the "thank-you" subject line.

Imagine you are a professional who opens his Inbox to find an e-mail with the subject line,

"Thank you for your great help last Thursday 08/27/2014"

Are you going to open one of the other e-mails which probably contain only work-related material, or are you going to open the thank-you e-mail first to find out what nice things the sender had to say about you?

More about the "thank-you"-email in a later chapter.

#4 – THE GREETING

Quite uncreatively the majority of all e-mails begin either with the universal greeting "hi" or no greeting at all.

Surely you have seen some if these funny videos titled "Facebook in Real Life," which show people randomly poking each other and writing on each others' office walls (available on Youtube). The same concept can be applied to e-mails as well.

Not offering a greeting is the equivalent of opening the door to somebody's office and saying, "I need this or that..." The effect is only slightly better when somebody opens the door and says, "Hi, I need this or that."

Nobody in his right mind would do that. 99% of people would say, "Good morning (name), How are you? Do you have a second? I wanted to ask you something about the xyz-project..." or something to that effect.

Obviously, it's a bit different when you write an e-mail. You don't need to ask if the recipient has time to address the issue because he will read the e-mail when he has time to handle it or when he wants to handle it. Still, that does not mean that all other polite phrases should be dropped, too.

Typing a polite, classy greeting sets the tone and will help you to build an excellent reputation.

"Good morning, Professor xyz. Please find my term paper "(title)" attached. As always, John Smith"

Other classy greetings are

- Dear

- Good Morning

- Good Afternoon

- Happy Holidays (Happy Easter, Happy Thanksgiving, etc.)

- Happy Spring Beginning!

- Greetings All (group e-mail)

If it applies, consider thanking your recipient right away, in the first sentence of your e-mail.

Here are the opening lines of an e-mail I wrote, which was very well received.

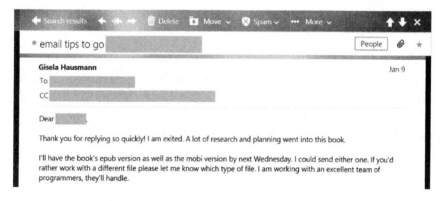

In a world where 100 billion e-mails are being sent every day, a quick response is something to be thankful for.

Notice how I raise the level of communication by writing, "I am excited." Expressing your feelings in a positive and professional tone will lead to your e-mails being more appealing than canned, pieced-together e-mails. Make an effort of doing it at the beginning of the e-mail.

Even though I recommend avoiding using the greeting "hi," sometimes it can be the best option.

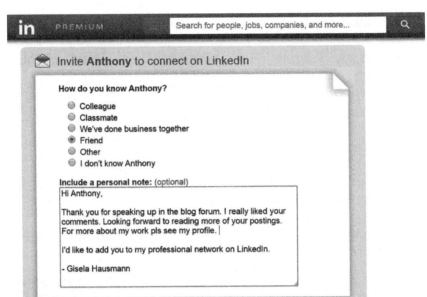

Invite **Anthony** to connect on LinkedIn

How do you know Anthony?

- Colleague
- Classmate
- We've done business together
- ● Friend
- Other
- I don't know Anthony

Include a personal note: (optional)

Hi Anthony,

Thank you for speaking up in the blog forum. I really liked your comments. Looking forward to reading more of your postings. For more about my work pls see my profile. |

I'd like to add you to my professional network on LinkedIn.

- Gisela Hausmann

If you are contacting somebody on Linkedin, your initial e-mail is limited to 400 characters. Under these circumstances "hi" is most likely the best greeting. Instead of skipping the "thank-you," you should elect to write "hi" because it takes up only two characters.

#5 – THE SPELLING OF THE RECIPIENT'S NAME

There is no faster way to say "I don't really care about you…" than misspelling a person's name. We identify with our names; consequently when we see people misspell our names, we conclude that they do not *really* care about us. And, should the e-mail come from a new contact, not spelling the recipient's name correctly indicates that the sender is sloppy; probably because he doesn't care.

In contrast to the last century, when parents often named their first born son after his father and their first born daughter after her grandmother, today many parents want to give their children a unique name, or at least make a more common name unique by giving it an alternate spelling.

This movement led to the popular girls' name Brianna also being spelled Briannah, Briana, Brienne, Brienna, and Breanne, with nickname versions Bree and Brea.

And, the popular boys' name Aiden is also being spelled Aidan, Aaden, Edan, and Adan.

My personal rule is, "If you must misspell a word in an e-mail, don't allow it to be a name (of a person or a company)."

People can be very understanding if they see a misspelled word; however, if that misspelled word is their own name, they suddenly don't think that the sender was in a hurry, or that his real strength lies in accounting (and not spelling), they think of the sender as a careless, disinterested person.

Also, in today's world of international communication, it is crucial to pay closest attention to the spelling of foreign names. To avoid possible mistakes, you might consider copying and pasting foreign names. To do this properly, you need to copy the person's name into a file that will strip any existing formatting (.txt). Only then paste the name from the .txt file into the e-mail. [All Microsoft Office programs keep the text's original formatting.]

The following e-mail illustrates what can happen if you do not strip the formatting. In this case the sender copied and pasted the e-mail's body from a MS word document into his e-mail and then added my name manually. How do I know?

The e-mail features two different fonts (notice the different font sizes). Since my name is misspelled, the sender could not have copied and pasted my name but had to have copied and pasted the body of the e-mail.

While the greeting ("Hello Gisella") is written in the font as defined by the sender's e-mail program settings, the body of the e-mail is displayed in a different font. This was caused by copying and pasting from a program that kept the original text's formatting.

Making this mistake is also one of the easiest ways for the recipient to find out that he received a mass e-mail.

Sending out e-mails that can be easily identified as mass e-mails invites the recipient to think, "I don't even need to consider this e-mail. Probably the sender sent the same e-mail to another 100 people. *Somebody else* is going to do it." => delete!

6 – THE BODY OF YOUR E-MAIL

Obviously, the content of e-mails can be vastly different, but the following three tips can be applied to all e-mails:

TIP 1: is probably the most important tip of this entire book: READ IMPORTANT E-MAILS OUT LOUD TO YOURSELF! Listen to yourself and decide, if the e-mail sounds polite, pleasant, and professional.

TIP 2: Check if you included all pertinent information. The reason for it is simple – Most people don't like to do things over.

If you forget to include pertinent information the recipient will have to send you an e-mail asking for the missing information. If that happens more than once, the recipient will think of you as an unorganized person.

On the other hand, if you always include all information the recipients of your e-mails will think of you as a highly organized person even if you keep "losing" socks every week.

You can buy socks but you can't buy a reputation. Sending first-rate e-mails is one part of building an excellent reputation.

TIP 3: Also, before sending very important e-mails, get some distance! Leave your desk! Maybe you want to get a glass of water or maybe take a stroll around your house or building. The idea is that you get your blood flowing and at the same time you clear your mind by looking at some different scenery. Then, take a last look at your e-mail, read it out loud one more time, and only then, once you have re-verified that it is the best it can be, send it off!

As long as you are in school or college your teachers, professors, counselors, and the administrators will always read your e-mails.

But, when you apply for an internship or a job, it is a completely different situation. Obviously, the recipient wants to hire the best interns or employees. That implies your e-mail competes with the e-mails of the other applicants.

Opposite to your teachers, who have a vested interest in you succeeding, other companies' employees are vested in their own companies' success. If you apply for a summer job the human resources specialist will examine your e-mail to see if it suggests that you will be a good fit for their company. In other words it's about the work or the project and NOT about you.

The basic idea is that the company wants to find an intern or an employee who is really interested in the specific work he is supposed to do at this company.

Let me explain with an example. This professional is trying to sell my company a service.

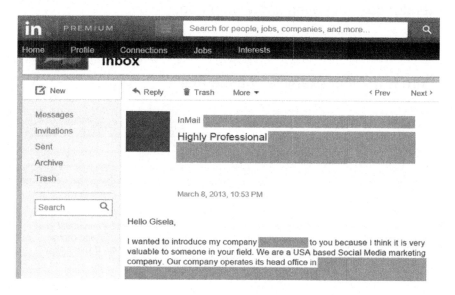

Reading this e-mail you will notice that it is what I call a ME-mail. It's all about the sender.

The sender begins by writing, "I wanted to introduce my company..."

Reading this sentence I think, "It's nice that you want to introduce your company but WHY should I care..."

Then, the sender writes, "I think it is very valuable...."

I think, "Maybe it isn't. Everybody wants to sell something. Everybody says that his stuff is valuable."

Finally, the sender writes, "someone in your field."

I think, "Someone? – And, which field?

Clearly, the sender is sending a mass e-mail to dozens if not hundreds of recipients, fishing for business.

To be successful this sender would have had to tell me, why my company or I need what he has offer; but apparently this sender does not even know what I do.

This is a "me-me-me - buy my stuff"-email.

Here is another example of a me-mail.

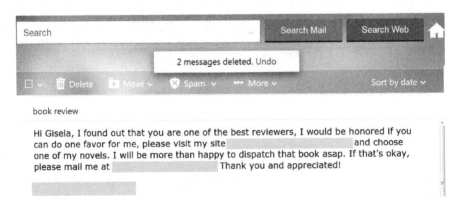

This sender (an author) wants me to read and review one of his books. Check how he went about it.

He writes, "I found out that you are..."

Reading this line I think, "You are not telling me anything new. I know who I am."

The sender writes, "I would be honored..."

I think, "Flattery!!!"

The sender writes, "... you can do **me** one favor..."

I think, "Everybody needs a favor."

And, the e-mail goes on and on. But, look **what's missing**.

This sender did not even write one line about what kind of books he writes. Fiction? Non-fiction? Love stories? Horror? Historical drama?

That would be the essential information a book reviewer really wants to know. Of course I could look up his website, but shouldn't the sender tell me why I would/could/should be interested in reading his book other than that he would be honored if I read it?

Request e-mails need to present the answers to questions like:

- "Why should I be interested in your product or service?"
- "Why should I read your book?"
- "Why should I hire you?"
- "Why should I feature your event on TV?"
- "Why should I finance your start-up?"
- and so on...

In other words, you must make your case why a recipient should be interested in your cause.

Here is how you can make sure that you are not sending a me-mail.

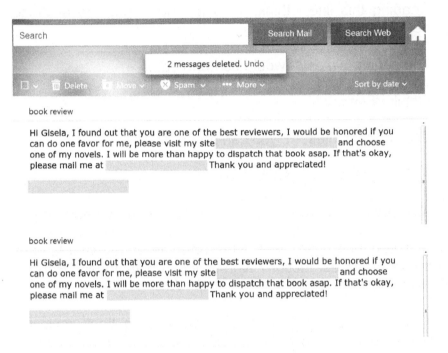

After typing your e-mail in a word document, highlight every instance of the words "I", "my", and "me." This particular e-mail has two of these words in almost every line.

7 out of 60 words, or 11.66% of all words are "I, my, me"-words. Clearly, this e-mail is all about the sender.

To write effective e-mails, never ever begin an e-mail with the word "I" and try to replace as many "I"s with "you"s as possible. In this case, the sender could have written, "You will enjoy reading my novel because..."

That's where research comes in.

The writer of the previous e-mail should have researched my reviewer record to see if I even read books of the genre he writes. If I don't there is no need to contact me, unless he can come up with a really good reason.

Before you apply for any job or internship check out the company's website.

Here is another somewhat embarrassing example:

Simply googling "Readers Favorite Award" would have led the sender of this e-mail to the website www.readersfavorite.com.

Most often googling information takes less than one minute. Repairing the impression that a sender is lazy or worse, that he does not know how search engines work, will take a lot longer.

Always keep in mind: We write e-mails to help the recipients (find best employees, interns, or products), to give them information, or to make them happy (thank-you e-mails).

At the same time, you must realize that everybody wants to get "great e-mails."

Every company is looking for best interns and best employees so they can grow and become a better company who produces better products or services.

Every news anchor, radio host, and podcast host wants to know what's new and noteworthy! That's their job! Therefore, if what you do is new and noteworthy please tell them! They will be grateful!

Absolutely everybody likes to receive thank-you e-mails.

And lastly, most successful people want to give back! Every influencer remembers the time when he was your age. As stated in the beginning of this book, achieving success is a team effort. Most often people, who are at the top like to help somebody just like they got help when they were your age.

It's up to you to make your case!

7 – THE ENDING SALUTATION & SIGNATURE

The ending salutation too is a terrific opportunity to distinguish your e-mail from most of the other e-mails in your recipient's Inbox.

Most people present the same old - same old ending salutation. They write "Sincerely," "Thanks," or "Thank you."

That implies, if you use any other ending salutation your e-mail will look more remarkable than the next person's.

As a general rule, never again use the ending salutation "Sincerely" – never, ever! My daughter once quipped very brilliantly: "Is there anything less sincere than sincerely... I sincerely doubt it..."

"Sincerely" is the most overused word in all e-mails – worldwide. It was first recorded as a subscription to letters in 1702. Since then it has become overused, uncreative, and boring. And, who wants to be boring?

Of course, you know that all great brands have their slogans. Similarly you can use the ending salutation like a slogan for your own brand.

Always keep in mind who you are sending the e-mail to before selecting an ending salutation.

"Official business e-mails" e.g. anything related to school, college, or an employment requires a more formal or most formal salutation, whereas the members of your school club would probably enjoy reading a humorous ending salutation.

Here is a good list to pick from:

Formal ending salutations:

- Thank you for your consideration,

- Yours respectfully,

- Respectfully yours,

- With anticipation,

- Confidently yours,

- Enthusiastically,

-

Informal, funny, and movie-quote ending salutations,

- May the gods guard your well being,

- Only you can prevent forest fires,

- Confusion to our enemies,

- Made in America, (or wherever)

- and that's all I have to say about that ("Forest Gump")

- May the force be with you, ("Star Wars")

- Live long and prosper, ("Star Trek")

- Color Outside the lines,

- Shine on,

- Keep on rollin in the free world,

- Unquestioningly,

- so as it is written, let it be done,

- This message will self destruct in 10 seconds,

Lastly, ALWAYS sign with your name. At social media platforms or when texting, we do not sign our messages because they are displayed next to our avatar. This has led to the bad habit of many people not signing their e-mails.

Even though your e-mail signature includes your name always type your name under your e-mail. It is more personal and helps build better business relationships.

Also, you should be proud of your name/your brand! "Signing" your e-mail expresses that pride.

(Sadly, there are people who claim they are too busy to type their own name. I believe that most of us can type their own name in under five seconds.)

THE PROBLEM WITH TEMPLATES

Maybe you are wondering why this book does not include any templates.

template *[tem-plit]* noun
: anything that determines or serves as a pattern; a model

(There are also other uses and definitions)

It is for the same reason as what's going on at schools, worldwide.

Of course, you know what happens when you send in your home work. Teachers run your work through a program which checks for plagiarism. Every student is supposed to deliver "original thoughts" or "original content," meaning YOU created it.

In the professional world, many people use templates when they apply for jobs. Typically, they search for templates on Google. There is also a saying, "you know you are trouble when your search leads you to page 2 on google," meaning that most people use the information they find on page 1 of their Google search.

These days very often 100+ people apply for the same job.

Can you imagine how many almost identical cover letters human resources experts get to see simply because a majority of people picked the same template? These applicants would not get by your teacher; do you think that they'll get the job?

However, it needs to stated that the problem isn't that people use a template, the problem is that too many people use **the same templates**.

Naturally you don't want to create the same content over again, when you apply for more than one job, or if you contact more than one media outlet. Therefore the best way to go is to create your *own* original template, and work with this "personal template."

If you know that you are going to look for an internship in the summer, you can begin creating a really cool template for your cover letter three months prior. Then, you can "test" this template by showing it to your parents, or a teacher, or other influential people.

Remember to use the template as a basis and then "tailor" your e-mail for the specific purpose.

Finally - don't give your template to others, unless you want to start a business writing cover letters or e-mails for others.

TYPOS, MISSPELLINGS, & THE MOST INFAMOUS WRITING ERROR

Since I am an author, I spend lot of time with other authors, publishers, and book reviewers. In these circles, people talk a lot about typos and how terrible typos and misspellings are. Many of my friends in the publishing industry think that anybody who makes typos and misspellings cannot be taken seriously.

In general, I believe that a well-crafted MESSAGE is far more important than knowing the rules for comma usage by heart.

That is why I advocate that everybody needs to know how to spell the words which pertain to his/her career.

If you want to be an animal keeper at a zoo, you need to know how to spell 'tortoise' correctly because sooner or later it'll come out. Anybody who misspells this word won't look like "on the career path to zoo director. "

If you want to be a chef, it can make a difference to know that 'schnitzel cordon bleu' contains the rare s - c - h combination; because it is an Austrian word, and 'cordon bleu' is a French word.

Obviously, it makes sense to learn what matters to your life; therefore you should look up these words and study them. Having a sophisticated vocabulary will put you on the track to management.

Beyond that, bad spelling errors and abbreviated spellings like it would be used on twitter or when texting should be avoided because it never looks good, as illustrated in the following example:

Dear Gisela,

Thank you for ur reply.

Ur idea sounds really good, I will think of making some more market research and convert my dissertation into an ebook...that would be very beneficial for my person...my name would be more recognisable ;)

Anyway, I reckon u r a very busy person...but if you want, I could send you a set of questions I am addressing to various individuals about their reading experiences and views on print/ebook. It's ten questions which need descriptive answering ;)

Anyway, if you don't want to get involved, that is absolutely fine :)

I appreciate ur help already :)

Thanks a lot for everything.

Let me know what do you think of that.

Looking forward to hearing from you.

Best wishes,

(name)

[Yes, I too wondered which college this student attends.]

***

Finally, there the three words which I most often see being used incorrectly:

- Your
- You're
- You are

Since these words are basic and they are taught in elementary school, using them incorrectly is worse than mixing up "adverse and averse" or "criteria and criterion."

Instead of writing "You're welcome", you could proclaim "It's been my pleasure". Spell check will correct any misspellings in this phrase, whereas it won't correct "your" or "you're" when either one is applied incorrectly.

EXCEPTION: Never misspell a recipient's name. Misspelling somebody's name indicates that you don't care about this person.

THE THANK-YOU E-MAIL

As a general rule – Thank everybody!

Writing a "thank-you" e-mail means that you are taking the time to say that the preceding events mattered in your life. That is everybody's goal. Everybody wants to do something that matters.

Therefore, thank the college counselor who helped you find information.

Thank the HR-person after you interviewed for a job.

Thank the graduate student who shared valuable information.

– And, put it in black on white!

Remember the chapter about "building your name"? Thanking everybody who helped you will help you to build a great name for yourself.

Most people work extremely hard and receive little thanks. Being the person who thanks them elevates you to becoming that special person whose e-mails everybody wants to open and read.

ONE LAST WORD

E-mails are legal documents and having to provide e-mail records is a standard procedure of full disclosure in legal cases. It implies that, sometimes, an e-mail that you wrote in haste might be read in court in the future, even if you never did anything wrong. Additionally, e-mail accounts sometimes get hacked. On the off chance that this happens to you or at an organization where you work, you always want to make sure that your e-mail is the one that sounds best.

Please note: Considering the fight against terrorism, the laws may be broadened and may also include information stored in clouds.

***

17 EXAMPLES OF LUDICROUS E-MAILS

This chapter wants to encourage you to go for the top. Regardless, how you rank your e-mail writing skills, there are people who could learn from you. Here are a few of their e-mails.

My annotations and thoughts are noted in brackets [...] underneath.

TOO SHORT, UNPROFESSIONAL E-MAILS

***

"Thanks honey,..."

[No, it is not cute.]

***

"That is fine."
(organization's signature block but no sender's name)

[No greeting, no name... In other words, it's NOT fine.]

***

"Hello,
Would you be interested in reviewing the ...xyz-Kit?
If so please send me you address and i will get it rite over to you. Thanks!" (no name)

[It is hard to believe that this e-mail comes from a marketing person of any US company.]

***

***

Yourr scanned documents cannot be printed. Fax them to
me at xxx-xxx-xxxx

*[No greeting, typo in the first word, and commanding tone…
from the secretary of a lawyer's office. It must be really hard
to find good help.]*

***

BS E-MAILS

[BS e-mails are e-mails that don't say anything; they have no real message.]

***

"Thank you, and the same to you." (no greeting, no salutation, no signature)

[That's all?]

***

Thanks for sharing this, Gisela. Really interesting stuff! (no greeting, no signature)

[Platitude]

***

Thank you Gisela for your involved concern. I will follow your advice. And of course seek further advice

[No greeting, no signature, and what exactly are you trying to say?]

***

Your valuable comments are most welcome…trust me, it matters a lot to me.
Warm personal Regards,

[No greeting, no signature. Is there a message in this array of catch phrases?]

***

As we approach the 228th anniversary of Declaration of Independence in USA we ask all concerned citizens to consider this Declaration of (...) as a (...)
And a four figure matching contribution continues the effort. Perhaps one of You are acquainted with a (...) Investor to whom a qualified executive briefing for this campaign can be attractive.
(name)

[? ? ? (Although it's is hard to believe, the writer is an American.)]

Hey Gisela,
Really appreciate you becoming part of my growing network of positive influencers. I like to spend a few minutes getting to know more about the people that choose to become my network. I would love to find out if there are any ways I can help support your life dreams, either now or in the future. When works to schedule a quick introductory call?

Have a lovely Sunday,
(no signature)

[a) Don't call me "hey" plus b) I doubt that anybody who doesn't know that 'hey' is not an appropriate greeting can support my life dreams, either now or in the future.]

CRAZY E-MAILS

***

Thanks babe x (no greeting, no sig)

[?]

***

Thank you for your prompt reply.
Could you send me e-mail addresses of Oprah Winfrey or some other internationally acclaimed philanthropist or evangelists.

[No greeting, no signature, plus I wonder if personal friends of Oprah or 'some other internationally acclaimed philanthropist or evangelist' would reply to this e-mail.]

***

TOO MUCH OR TOO LITTLE INFORMATION E-MAILS

***

(No greeting)
I just realized I mistyped your e-mail address on the instructions I just sent.
Hope you have a great week.
(no signature, but a religious quote in lieu of a signature)

[Sent by a paralegal. (She no longer works at that office.)]

***

(no greeting)
The power of coaching and self-coaching. 2015 is ours! Let's ROCK! In this blog post (almost 4K words, I spent the whole morning writing it for you) I share my best strategies, steps for success and fulfillment as well as the best health, wealth, business and happiness coaching resources. Enjoy! (no signature)

[Does anybody really believe you wrote it in one morning? And, if you did write 4K words in one morning, can this blog be good? Professional writers need longer to write 4K words.]

***

Considering your success with books as well as your publishing background, I was looking to see if you would be interested in publishing these two great children's books which I have written. I have been wanting to publish these books for a long time.
Regards, (signature)

[No greeting, no info – What makes 'these books' great? Plus, sorry to break your bubble, but all of us want something.]

***

Hi Gisela,
Thank you for the connection...we are in the development process of a feature film here in the NE US area and are looking for funding. If you or someone you know may be interested in hearing more please let me know.
beautiful name by the way!
(signature)

[48 words – absolutely no effort! What kind of feature film? Low-budget? Sci-fi? The difference could be in the millions of dollars. Also, do you always ask people who you don't know too well for money?]

***

okey dokey, coming your way, but expect a delay as I am between shipments
right now.
thx many times Gisela.
(Initials)

[No greeting, plus the writer never shipped the book, which did not really come as a surprise after reading that e-mail.]

***

TEEN ENTREPRENEURS DO AMAZING THINGS

A few teen entrepreneurs' websites:

*

http://www.man-cans.com

13-year-old Richard "Hart" Main was wondering why there weren't any candles for men, which smelled like a new leather baseball mitt or like sawdust. So, he invented them, and he is helping to feed hungry people too.

*

http://www.braigolabs.com

LEGO enthusiast Shubham Banerjee, a 12-year-old middle school student from Santa Clara, invented an open source cost reduced DIY braille printer for the visually impaired.

*

http://www.cellphonesforsoldiers.com/in_the_press.php

Teenagers Robbie and Brittany Bergquist from Norwell, MA started "Cell Phones for Soldiers" with $21 of their own money.

*

TWEETS from the #EmailEvangelist

As you arrive at the end of this book I am inviting you to

CALL FOR BETTER E-MAILS.

You probably receive some pretty bad ones too.

These are some of my #EmailEvangelist tweets. Find the ones that speak to you and blast them out into the twitter universe. All of these tweets have less than 110 characters. If you add #EmailEvangelist I'll tweet right back.

☆

It's not an Inbox problem;
it's an email problem.

☆

You must write the email you wish others will
read.

☆

Struggle not to write a bestseller but rather an
email that matters.
Success will follow by itself.

☆

They call it email, because me-mail was too long.

☆

Your knowledge writes the email.
Your brains signal 'send'.

*

Until you have lost an email, you never realize
what value it represents,
having it in black and white.

*

To find out your real opinion of someone,
judge the impression you have
when you first see an email from them.

*

Your knowledge writes the email.
Your brains signal 'send'.

*

To me, some emails read like somebody
wrote a love letter to himself.

*

Many emails are like the shock
produced by a freezing cold bath.

*

'Classic.'
An email which people talk about in staff meetings
and don't read.

*

There's only one email strategy: Be concise!

*

A template for everybody is an email to nobody.

*

Emails speak louder than phone calls.

*

Emails have no limitations,
except the ones you don't write.

*

This is not an email but my thoughts focusing on
what you need,
for a brief moment.

*

The present email is a very long one,
simply because I had no leisure to make it shorter.

This is not an email but my thoughts wrapped
around you
for a brief moment.

*

Following the promise of an email, we left the Old
World.

*

Don't count the emails, make the email count.

~~*~~

THANK YOU for buying
NAKED TEXT
Email-Writing for Teenagers

Please leave a review at Amazon.com – It helps authors
to find out what readers would like to read more of.

***

To find out about upcoming 'naked books'
please subscribe at
**http://www.giselahausmann.com/free-creative-
ideas.html**
You will also receive one creative idea per week.
Please know that this author is an e-mail evangelist.
I value and respect subscribers and will not inundate you
with sales e-mails.

***

Please connect with me

http://www.giselahausmann.com/contact.html

More books by Gisela Hausmann

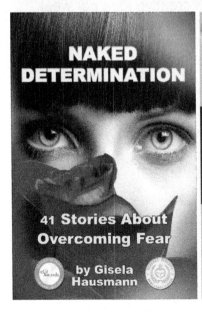

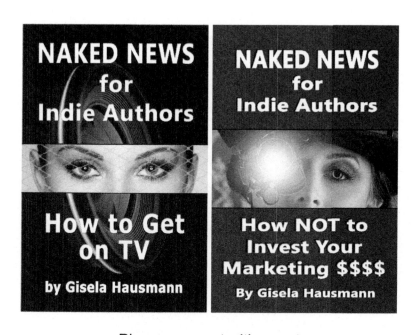

Please connect with me at
http://www.giselahausmann.com/

About the Author

Gisela Hausmann is a marketing and mass media expert.

She is also an email evangelist.

The author of nineteen books, she publishes books under her "naked" brand of books, meaning Gisela publishes "no-fluff" books.

Born to be an adventurer, Gisela has also co-piloted single-engine planes, produced movies, and worked in the industries of education, construction, and international transportation. Gisela's friends and fans know her as a woman who goes out to seek the unusual and rare adventure.

A unique mixture of wild risk-taker and careful planner, Gisela globe-trotted almost 100,000 kilometers on three continents, including to the locations of her favorite books: Doctor Zhivago's Russia, Heinrich Harrer's Tibet, and Genghis Khan's Mongolia.

Gisela Hausmann graduated with a master's degree in Film & Mass Media from the University of Vienna. She now lives in Greenville, South Carolina.

***

Notes:

Notes:

Notes:

Notes: